CELEBRATING MY NEW WALK

LAWRENCE VICKSTROM

ISBN-13: 978-1977843616
ISBN-10: 1977843611

Publishing

Lighthouse International Ministries
MPO Box 2813
Niagara Falls, New York
14302

INTRODUCTION

I want to start this out by Giving God thanks for all He has saved me from. Today I am a Foot Washer in Gods kingdom. I help feed, clothe and home the local homeless. I feel now in my life I am doing what God has called me to do. This has been such a long road to get me this far.

Ephesians 2:8-10

For by grace you have been saved through faith. And this is not your own
doing; it is the gift of God, not a result of works, so that no one may boast. For we are his workmanship, created in Christ Jesus for good works, which God prepared beforehand, that we should walk in them.

As a child, I never knew the love of a father. My real father was a skate partner of my mother. On the way home one night, he did the unthinkable to my mother, I was made. He then went to the Marines,

He never came back on any of his leave's so they divorced.
My mother then remarried someone That turned out to be worse than her first husband. He was only a part of our lives a brief time before he spent 20 years in prison. In the time that he was a part of our lives, my mother gave birth to 2 siblings and was pregnant with another when arrested.

We moved to Westland, Michigan, and after my stepfather's arrest, my mother started going to church. The church we went to was very close and loving. Just like family. My mother started getting real close to God. We always had a house full of people that fell on their luck. My mom would take them in. She always wanted to help everyone who was in need. I guess that is where I get it from.

One night, my Aunt brought home a man. He wanted to have sex with her and she turned him down. When she fell asleep, he found his way to my room and raped me.

I was only 11 now in my life.
This changed my whole outlook on life since he went to our church. This only happened once with him, but I started having trust

issues, and it planted the seed of sex in my mind.
This would not be the last time I am raped, it would happen two more times and it left me very mixed up and tore up.

We started to move a lot so this made it very hard to make friends. We moved from that home and two hours from our church. We moved closer to the prison where my Stepfather was at.

By this time, I was mixed up and I started to steal porn from the store. This fed my mind. I really started acting out. I started stealing more, getting bad grades, lying, wetting the bed, breaking toys, and hurting myself.

For the first time ever at the age of 13 I saw my real father. He came over to blow up on me for my bad grades. This was the last time I saw him until I was 18.

My love for porn and sex took over my life. The first girl I thought I loved and wanted to have sex with at the age of 15. I could not even go through the act. From that day on, I would just block my feelings.

Sex outweighed love.

At the age of 16, my mother re-married again. We moved to northern Michigan, and this is where I find myself involved with drinking, doing drugs, playing pool, and hanging out in bars, meeting all the wrong people at an early age.

This helped me find easy women. I finished school at the age of 18, and I moved to Fort Lauderdale wanting to get to know my real father and this was short-lived.

I found myself in the punk scene, at this point, I found out about PCP. My life went out of control and moved place to place for a while.

I ended up back in Michigan in a small town called Flat Rock.

I moved in with my aunt. That did not last long, I met a woman that would later give birth to my oldest daughter.

My life once again fell out of control I found myself hanging out with a gang, dealing drugs, and carrying a gun.

I confused in everything I did and had no hope in my life.

After my little girl was born, I tried to hold down a job and do the right thing, but drugs had too much of a hold on my life.

I went over to see my child one day and was told to stay away from my girlfriend and child or I would be buried under the front porch of their home. I left there wanting to end it all.

I found myself on an overpass high and drunk looking down over the cars wanting to just die. I stood there and my feet would not leave the rail as tears filled my eyes. I heard a voice to call my aunt, somehow, I found a payphone, I made the call and she told me that she had been praying for me for three days.

Ephesians 2:1-22
And you were dead in the trespasses and sins in which you once walked, following the course of this world, following the prince of the power of the air, the spirit that is now at work in the sons of disobedience—

among whom we all once lived in the passions of our flesh, carrying out the desires of the body and the mind, and were by nature children of wrath, like the rest of mankind. But God, being rich in mercy, because of the great love with which he loved us, even when we were dead in our trespasses, made us alive together with Christ—by grace you have been saved— ...

My Aunt told me about a program called teen challenge. This program taught me so much about the bible and Jesus. I stayed in the program for 3 years. After 2 1/2 years, I could stay in a staff house but I had to find a church and report back to the center daily.

I found a church and this is where I met my ex-wife. Once again sex took over my life and she became pregnant with our oldest boy before marriage.

On our honeymoon, we came to Florida and I left her at my parents for a week while I got high and cheated on her.

My wife was pregnant once again.

We ended up working things out and I went to work off shore as a Chef. The money was great but the life style was not.

Being gone off shore and living the life I did tore our marriage apart. Both of us were very unhappy and cheated on each other. We devoiced.

Once again, I found myself drinking and on PCP back in Detroit. Found another woman and we lived together and she became pregnant. At this point I talked her into adopting the child to someone else. After she did that, I got deeper into drugs.

I was sitting in my living room one night and heard a lot   of yelling outside my door. I opened it with   my cell phone in my hand and saw the police officers dragging my friend down the stairs. I turned on the camera and told them I was filming them. They told me if I did not want some I better go back inside. I went to the front of the building to tell my girlfriend to come in and by the time I told her the police came around and saw me. I woke up in the hospital, was in ICU for a month, almost died. After leaving the hospital, I moved to Florida.

To only have the girl I was trying to leave

trail right behind me. Once again drinking and drugs took over my life. Two years go by and she leaves me for someone else. I find myself once again wanting to end it all, with a gun in my mouth, that jams and does not go off. The next day, my stepfather buys it from me.

2Timothy 4:18
The Lord will rescue me from every evil deed and bring me safely into his heavenly kingdom. To him be the glory forever and ever. Amen.

I find myself on the rebound with a woman with five children. I found a wonderful job and worked too much. I had nothing to show for it but a video game that took up all my spare time. Then once again porn finding its way back in my life. On the computer it was easy for me to stare at porn.

For 10 years gaming, porn and working ran my life. It got to a point I hid myself in a walk-in closet with a microwave and fridge where I could keep all I thought I needed.

I slipped and fell at work and tore my rotator cup which put me out of work.

Things started to fall apart and I moved back to Florida, down and out my and parents allow me to come home.

I started buying and selling things at a flea market and cooking for people that could not do it for themselves, started doing well and I met another woman.

We hit it off right away and things started off good, but soon my sickness with porn gets us with the Law at our door.

I decided one night to remove all my porn. I had 10 years of photos that I kept it on a storage website and they reported me to homeland security.

I was in handcuffs for four hours fearing to in prison forever. I put the woman I was with and her child in danger. They took my laptop and kept me in fear for a year and a half. After they told me they cleared me and I knew at once I had to stop the porn. The need to watch it was strong, so I did watch it every now and then but I was trying to do my best to stay away.

I started to read my Bible more and pray a lot. The woman and I broke up. I came up with some money and bought a home in Zephyrhills.

That brings me back to today, I can go on for hours on what God has done for me. The many blessings I see and the prayers that are answered in my life.

I am overcoming my PTSD with the help of a good friend that is a state trooper, I am a co-leader in a celebrate Recovery group,

I am in the Lamp program and learning to be a better person in Gods Kingdom. I am now putting my writings in book form with the help of Hannah House.

The I's in this Testimony is not the pride in me speaking out its knowing I can do anything with God in control.

The rest of this book is to uplift and guide others to overcome whatever you have going on in your life. I have not overcome everything. I am still living in God's grace and trying to reach my goals.

STEP #1

I admitted I was powerless over my addictions and compulsive behaviors, that my life had become unmanageable.

Romans 7:18
I know that nothing good lives in me, that is, in my sinful nature. For I have the desire to do what is good, but I cannot carry it out.

We are in pain, and for some of us the pain never leaves We are angry, it is like a ticking time, bomb just waiting for someone to set us off We are sad, watching as life goes on while we cannot find the will to stand. We fight our demons, disorders and conditions that try to hold us down We hide our tears, pretending everything will be all right We are hurting, and some days it feels like we'll never heal. We are broken. But that does not define us. We are in pain, but that pain is sometimes being outshined by the love of our friends,

We are angry, but each day we work to let go and forgive. We are sad, but at the dawn of the new day we pick ourselves up again and try We fight our demons, and sometimes we even win We hide our tears, but those tears are sometimes happy as those we love help mend our hearts We are hurting, but through that we can connect to others and lift them up as they fight to become something more.

STEP # 2

I came to believe that a power greater than ourselves could restore Me to sanity.

Philippians 2:13
For it is God who works in you to will and to act according to his good purpose.

The reason?
4 years ago, I had lost hope, all parts of myself, like a blank slate and complete mess at the same time.

But it was He that reminded me who I was.

11 years ago, I stood in my kitchen holding a gun to my head, thinking that metal would be my salvation, but He whispered to me, "That is not what you're here for.

"There were times where I couldn't even hear a whisper.

My doubts enveloped me with vicious vigor, yet my downcast soul still held some light.

It was still willing to fight for what is right.

Little did I know that in my plight God was already bringing me back to life, pushing away darkness with light, despair with hope, sickness with healing. Slowly breaking barriers, lies I told myself and drowned in, insecurities I could never conquer on my own strength.

When I stood in His presence,
emotion was poured back into my
bones, so I know He lives, He is here.

For how could an apathetic and
depressed soul like mine feel anything,
having been drained by my mistakes
and regrets and a life I thought was
too terrible to even bother with?

And yet even when I did not feel
anything, when I imagined my body
as a shell, looking up at humanity from
my glass prison, I still felt Him.

The still, small voice penetrated
Through My brain, He whispered,
"You will endure."

And I said "God, you tell me you have
plans for me, that this is not the end of
my story, but I cannot see! I can't see
it."

In my cage was only silence and
darkness, I could not see that there
was also God's goodness, His

intervention.

Because during this darkness,
He gave me my purpose: He gave me
words.

A calling, the Holy Spirit pound, pound,
pounding the life back into my heart
with every word I typed.

He gave me words, stories, He gave
Me a voice.

My world was no longer silent, but
Filled with the hope of existence.

He gave me an outlet for what was
inside me, and I did not realize then
that he was guiding me.

Words used to be my greatest enemy,
my tongue locked by social anxiety,
my hands making illegible scribbling.

All I had wanted to do was sing an
empty song and gain empty riches.

But the Lord showed me what my real passion is.

Out of my deep slumber came a purpose, a stream of light—a constellation of clarity: Out of my nothingness God made the best part of me.

The one that can glorify Him with my mind, my soul, my body.

I am the lost sheep, rid of guilt, unbound from shame, known in identity as a son of the undoubtedly living, true God.

With Christ I have meaning. Through Him, I love.

He transcends even the most shattered of hearts into works of beautiful art. So, I will pen on the page, Jesus is Lord!

I will type in all caps, PRAISE THE LORD!

I will shout to the skies, God is alive!

Because He saved me.

Not just on the cross.

I believe in Jesus because He saved me from my misery.

I believe that apart from God, we cannot do anything.

STEP # 3

I decided to turn my life and my will over to the care of God.

Romans 12:1
Therefore, I urge you, brothers, in view of God's mercy, to offer your bodies as living sacrifices, holy and pleasing to God - this is your spiritual act of worship.

God used to be easier when his views fit my own, when he affirmed what I already believed, when he moved

within my stereotypes, proved right
what I already knew.

God used to be easier when my
enemies were His, when He affirmed
my prejudice, when He approved of the
boundaries drawn up between "us" and
"them".

God used to live in this comfortable
box of the culture I knew and the
worldview I treasured, among people I
loved who thought just like me.

But now You have opened the box and
He runs wild and free, challenging me
and who I thought He is.

This God questions my long-
held beliefs, challenges all I thought I
knew, tears down my prejudices and
will not let me be the way I used to be.
Now God is teaching me to touch those
who once disgusted me, to love those I
looked down upon, to open my heart to
the ones I rejected, to open my eyes to
wounds I was blind to see, to embrace

those who once were repulsive to me.
For you touch the lepers, you eat with
sinners, you mingle with rabble,
commune with foreigners.

You show me the God I have
misunderstood, the God I only saw
through my own clouded lenses that
sought confirmation of my distaste
instead of seeking truth.

So, let me follow You, my Lord,
overcoming all hatred, disgust and fear.

Let me follow You, my Lord, my God
who questions me.

STEP # 4

I made a searching and fearless moral inventory of ourselves.

Lamentations 3:40
Let us examine our ways and test them, and let us return to the Lord.

My day to day fight with my addiction, the things I fight with daily wanting to change my ways but sometimes the urge is stronger than my wellbeing and I know I cannot do this alone, my faith in my upper power is what keeps me over powering my addiction and keeps me coming back one more day.......

Addiction is where you cannot let go of something.

It starts off small, then increases in rate and intensity.

If you do not do it, you feel extremely anxious and you cannot focus.
You find a way to be alone so you can do it. For example, you will sit in the deserted stairwell at the roof level so you can get your fix.

Yet you hope for someone to discover you, because as strange as it sounds: You want to be by yourself, but you do not want to be alone.

At first people do not know, then they find out or you tell them straight up.

They interrogate you and take away your addiction by force. That makes you relieved at first, then angry at your next urge.

But your desire makes you suddenly creative and you discover 10 more ways to get the rush. You are always on your guard now.

You cannot trust them, nor they you. You dread a day when you are exposed again.

That is when you hear that you should give up your addiction.

Over and over.

You do not know if you can or even want to give it up.

Then one day, years later, you decide to get some help for it.

You try so very hard, but it is always in the back of your mind.

You dream about it.

You constantly think about it.

You have urges.

You even envision yourself getting fixes. You zone out when you see something that reminds you of it, where it is hard to come back to reality.

You tried alternatives, they did not work.
You sought support, they called you weak.
And you realized that quitting is exhausting.

You're just not cut out for this.
It keeps coming back.

You thought you were doing okay for a while.

You fail repeatedly.

Stumble after stumble.

Your will to quit wears thin.

You do not know why next time's attempt should result in anything but failure.

You get angry at yourself every time you do it.

You know it is easier to destroy yourself.

Every second is one more decision to make: Quit, or resume the habit.

STEP # 5

I admitted to God, to myself, and to another human being the exact nature of My wrongs.

James 5:16a
Therefore, confess your sins to each other and pray for each other so that you may be healed.

Time indeed flies' night and day,
Ready to run the race every day.
A purpose Christ gave us all to fulfill,
An essential one, to submit alone to His will.

A time came that joy, abundantly came and filled my heart, But one situation too many, stuck my soul like a fiery dart.

So painful and torturing, it left me a deeply wounded scar.

The devil will use anything to take advantage against us Christians,
Be it your weakness, your past, or even the worst tyrants.

Better not throw away that very precious and divine God-given blessing, if not careful, on the last day, we will find ourselves missing.

Back and forth, accusations flied, many
turned their back on me as I arrived,
Every day, I was tried and despised;
That at some point, I almost and
sometimes cried.

Tried to cast all fear aside, as some
think that I deserve to be fried.

Bondage is one of the devil's
dangerous weapons, Stinging souls
with fear, deceiving them with false
reasons.

Attacks came in, more than a times
pair, Suffocating, I felt like gasping for
air.

People looking at me with a
judging eye, Secretly labeling' me a liar
that deserves to go bye-bye.

Yet, upon every tearful plea, Out of His
love and mercy, God has forgiven me.
To all bullies roaming around out there,

You think you have just won it all fair and square?

But let me tell you this: you have not Won anything, what will you gain by committing this evil thing?

But now, I can no longer live in a condemning bondage, When Christ Jesus came in and broke my shackles.

As of now, I have nothing to fear at any age, Even though in future and present,I shall face all matter of troubles.

Call me stupid, crazy or dumb, But by His grace, I have move on, from bondage to freedom.

STEP # 6

I am entirely ready to have God remove all these defects of character.

Humble yourselves before the Lord, and he will lift you up.

Help me, the girl cries to an uncaring world around her.

Feeling.

Kill me, the man screams at the universal prank of his life.

Healing.

Save me, the boy sobs in the corner as his family tears itself apart.

Bleeding.

Love me, the woman says to every man she meets, looking for that one.
They are dying.

The smiles are melting, the disease slowly bleeding through.

The minds are healing, their sickness

wondrously cured.

While the hearts, left murdered on the streets, slowly rot away.

STEP # 7

I humbly asked Him to remove all my shortcomings.

1 John 1:9
If we confess our sins, he is faithful and will forgive us our sins and purify us from all unrighteousness.

My spirit is starving, all along I have been dying, Because I have not been reaching, And I have not been trying- I have only been wasting time, and crying, Now I am so dizzy, and my eyes are burning, Frozen like this, the worlds stopped turning, and all I can see, is their blood in my eyes, but heroes are not made, with hearts full of lies, I'm realizing now, I should save my own life, by ridding myself, Of the shame and the strife, I will leave it to Jesus, to do all the saving, as for me my spirit is craving, I have seen His love, in so many places- In the voice of my friends, my tears, their faces, reaching now, I have grabbed hold of His word, my grip is tighter this time, I will not be I will run strait this time, towards what deterred, I learned the hard way, that I cannot do this alone, I need help fighting what is real, and braving the unknown, I can feel you here now, I can tell that you are there, I know that you are listening, I know that you care, Now I know who I am, and who I want to be, Hear me, Lord,

As I fall to my knees:

I surrender to you!

My God, please!
Father, save me

Free me

And take me

STEP # 8

I made a list of all persons that had harmed and became willing to make amends to them all.

Luke 6:31
Do to others as you would have them do to you.

You see the tears and pain behind these eyes, you see the truth deep inside this mind, Betrayal runs within these veins, Running deep, numbing the pain.

They tied me up with their magic strings, they pinned me down and made me "sing".

They stole away what was mine to give, they tore me apart, made me regret; With another cut, I buried the pain.

With another scar, I hide the shame.

With another torch, I found the truth.

With another loss, I found my blame.

With another blade, I found my breath.

Betrayal lingers in my eyes, With the
pain I cannot seem to hide.

Memories haunt, memories steal, what
was mine to give, Was never real,
They stole my mind, Stole my freedom,
Stole my innocence, And the ability to
feel.

To feel much beyond this pain, to see
beyond the window pane.

They tied me up with magic strings,
Pinned me down and made me scream;
Tears welled up inside my eyes, they
stole my soul, they did not care, they
took what they wanted, they took what
was not theirs; They ripped me apart,
Inside and out, you think it is funny;
This thing called rape.

Stand one day in my shoes.
Then in mind sanely choose.

I am now working on forgiveness in my life I should be able to forgive to be forgiven, that is a challenging thing to deal with sometimes, Visions of the past flood my mind.

My heart begins to feel with sorrow and anger.

Things said or done in the past haunt me.

Can I forgive others for what they have done to me?

Sitting in a room full of people, I listen to their stories.

The stories are filled with hurt, pain and anger.

Their voices recall the deed that was done to them in volumes.

Can they not forgive others for what they have done to them?

Sitting in this room, stories and vision from time passed came to my heart.

These stories and visions came from a book that I hold dear.

These stories are of a man who walked this earth long ago.
In his journey of life, this man suffered many things done to him.

The vision that comes before me now, it is the vision of Jesus Christ our Savior.

While living on this earth, was he not disbelieved and persecuted for his way of life?

While living on this earth, did he not carry marks on his body from the whip?

While hanging on the cross, before he died, was he not made fun of by being called King of the Jew?

This man walking the earth, did he not forgive those who sought him?

This man teaching us about God our father, did he not forgive those who disbelieved?

This man who was scorned and beaten with a whip, did he not forgive those who transgressed against him?

This man carrying his own cross to Calvary, did he not say, "Father forgive them for they know not what they do."?

I FORGIVE YOU. I love you and hope the Lord Jesus will turn you from your evil ways and help you get the help you need in your life.

STEP # 9

I made direct amends to such people whenever possible, except when to do so, would injure them or others.

Matthew 5:23-24

Therefore, if you are offering your gift at the altar and there remember that your brother has something against you, leave your gift there in front of the altar. First go and be reconciled to your brother; then come and offer your gift.

Show Me.

I have heard the words so many times, before -do not say them all again.

They say that seeing is believing, so why don't you show me?

Not proof and archaeology, logic and theology, no science and no philosophy - show me living testimony.

Show me how you do it day by day,

how you read and how you pray,

how your Jesus made you new,

how his presence lives in you,

how you handle daily tasks,

how you do what your God asks,

how he answers when you pray,

and provides from day to day -Rather than telling me what to do, show me how you do it.

Rather than telling me what to believe, show me why I should.

Give me an example and I will follow.

STEP # 10

I continue to take personal inventory and when I were wrong, promptly admitted it.

1Corinthians 10:12
So, if you think you are standing firm, be careful that you don't fall!

I want you to imagine yourself in my place, in this vision:

Imagine yourself on a narrow road, as narrow as a side walk.

As you walk, all you see is extremely tall buildings at each of your sides, no way out.

Only way is to go forward, cause there is nothing but darkness behind you.

As you walk, you see Jesus so close and yet so far away.
You start seeing Demons in every window, taunting you, calling you names.

You begin to run to Jesus, but as you run, the Demons start throwing things at you, yelling at you.

As you get closer to Jesus, they start bringing up personal things from the past.

Then you hear something from one of them that really hurt you, something you did in the past.

When you get distracted, you trip and fall. When you're on the ground, you're both scared and sad.

Then you hear voices behind you, and they strike fear into your heart.

When you look back. You see this Angel being tore up and bitten by a Demon, and the Angel is shouting to you,
saying: Hey! Get up!

Start worshiping God, pray!

Run to Jesus!

If you don't do it, I will have no choice but to go back to heaven!

And that Demon will mess you up!

And he will drag you down to hell with him!

Get up!

Run!

But you are too afraid to move.

Then you hear Jesus' voice calmly say: Do it, before it is too late.

Then you begin to run inhumanly fast, getting so close to Jesus, almost there.

As you keep running, the Angel gets larger and stronger, and the more the Demons throw things at you.

Once you are only a few feet away from Jesus, every Demon jumps out of the buildings and forms a building sized Demon, Legion.

As soon as you are about to get to Jesus, Legion grabs your leg.

But you're not giving up, you're holding strong. You start fighting, and you reach Jesus.

Then Jesus wraps you in his arms.

Once there, the Legion Demon looks angry, but can do nothing, but just stand there and watch you receive your blessing.

Hebrews 12:1
Therefore, since we are surrounded by such a huge crowd of witnesses to the life of faith, let us strip off every weight that slows us down, especially the sin that so easily trips us up. And let us run with endurance the race God has set before us.

1 Corinthians 9:24

Do you not know that in a race all the runners run, but only one gets the prize? Run in such a way as to get the prize.

Matthew 14:30

but when he saw the strong wind and the waves, he was terrified and began to sink. "Save me, Lord!" he shouted. When peter was distracted and took his eyes off Jesus he fell too.

Ephesians 6:12

For we are not fighting against flesh-and-blood enemies, but against evil rulers and authorities of the unseen world, against mighty powers in this dark world, and against evil spirits in the heavenly places.

STEP # 11

I sought through prayer and meditation to improve

my conscious contact with God, praying only for knowledge of His will for me, and power to carry that out.

<u>Colossians 3:16a</u>
Let the word of Christ dwell in you richly.

Do you ever feel frustrated?

Do you feel like a lot of people just don't understand the concept that knowing God is about a relationship with an interactive being?

I am going to reflect on a few things that I have learned that have helped me understand this.

God is a real person.

He is a supernatural and divine person. He is God.

But He is a person.

The bible says God is a Spirit.

He is not just some spirit/universe energy floating around.

But He is a person. He has a form and personality.

"You mean God is like us?"

No!

YOU are like Him!

Genesis 1:26
God made you in His image and likeness. Not the other way around.

God is a spirit and you are a spirit.

God made man's body and breathed His spirit, put part of Himself, into you.

You are His offspring.

God has emotions. He does not let them control Him like we

sometimes do.

But He has them.

Is it possible then, that we could do something to positively touch Gods emotions?

First understand this; God loves you no matter what. God feels love towards you and He is eternally happy and pleased with you.

God is happy with you forever even if you mess up, because you are righteous due to Christ's obedience at the cross, not by your own obedience or actions.

And there is NOTHING that you could ever do to make God angry with you.

2 Corinthians 5:17
You can't save yourself, but now that you know Jesus, you are a New creation.

and when God looks at you, He sees the blood, Christ's blood, which covers you.

Jesus did this because He wants relationship with you. Jesus wants relationship with you because He loves you.

Look at

Acts 13:2
"As they ministered to the Lord, the Holy Spirit said, "Set apart for Me Barnabas and Saul for the work to which I have called them."

Look at that first part about ministering to the Lord.

When we "minister" to someone we are doing something good for them right?

Yeah, so is it possible to minister to God?

Apparently. Ministering to someone can be serving them or doing something nice for them, right?

Yes.
Also think about telling someone about Jesus.

Is telling someone about how amazingly awesome Jesus is, ministering to them?

Yes of course.

The truth of Jesus sets people free.

But is it possible, that
telling Jesus how amazingly awesome He is, is ministering to Him?

"Why would Jesus need us to tell Him how awesome He is?

Is He stupid?"

No.

That's not it.
But think about this; think about someone in a relationship with their husband/wife.

They like to hear "you're awesome" from each other, right?

You like to hear things like "You're awesome because...!"

from someone you love.

Jesus loves you.

Of course,
He would not expect you to
call Him awesome if you did not have a reason to.

But you do!
Look at

Psalm 35:27
"Let the Lord be magnified, who has pleasure in the prosperity of His servant".

Jesus delights in blessing you! That is awesome in itself! There is your first reason! And He is so much more! Jesus does not want your religion, He wants your relationship.

John 3:16
"For God so loved the world that He gave His only son so that whoever believes in him shall not die but have eternal life".

Let us take a closer look at what Jesus came to do for you.

Eternal life.

What is it?

Nobody ceases to exist.

So that's a given. The "eternal life" that Jesus won for you is much more than saving you from your sins so you could live forever in heaven one day.

That's part of it.

And that's great.

But it's not the main point of what He was trying to do.

There is more.

In

John 17
Jesus says eternal life is knowing God.

The word "know" that's used here is the same word that is used throughout the bible to describe an intimate relationship.

Jesus wants to enjoy a relationship with you.

If you love someone you want to be actively involved in their life, right?

You want to be with them.

Jesus not only wants to bless you

because that makes Him happy,

but He also wants to enjoy those blessings with you because He loves you and enjoys being with you.

The bible says that all things we are created for God's pleasure.

You are the object of affection of your God. In the Bible our relationship with Christ is the same as marriage.
Imagine a married couple.
They spend all day in the same house doing various things, but they never acknowledge each other's presence.

If one of them does decide to acknowledge the other one,
it's when one of them says "OK, I've decided that I'm going to talk to you for a certain period of time.

But after that its back to pretending like you're not here."

Sounds like a pretty troubled relationship, right?

The truth is, even if that couple was not "talking", if they would just acknowledge each other, their relationship would be a lot better.

Sometimes it's not even about conversing with the person, but just being with that person. If it is someone you really love, you enjoy just being in their presence, even if you are not saying anything.
You are ALWAYS in the presence of God. If you are in Christ, the Holy Spirit is in you. The Holy Spirit is God's Spirit living on earth today.

He is the one who is with you right now. Not just when you pray, but He is always with you. Even if you are not paying attention to Him, He is paying attention to you, working for you, speaking to you and doing things for you that you do not even notice.

You do not have to get his attention to talk to Him.

You have it.

Just start talking.

Prayer can be talking to Him, but even if you are not talking at all, that doesn't mean that you shouldn't acknowledge His presence.

He enjoys just being with you.

Tell Him that you know He's there. Comment to Him throughout the day.

He loves you!

If it bothers you, it bothers Jesus.

Luke 12:7
"...the very hairs on your head are all numbered. So, don't be afraid; you are more valuable to God than a whole flock of sparrows!"

Come on. Hairs?

Who cares?!?!

Jesus does.

Look, if your God cares enough that this detail is significant to Him, then nothing about your life is too insignificant for Him to pay attention to.

Something good?

Enjoy it with Him!

No matter how small.

"You know Jesus, this is a really good cupcake."

Or

"That guy was really funny wasn't he Jesus?"

Something bad?

Do not be afraid to bring it up, no matter how small or insignificant it seems to you.

He wants to take care of it.

Yes, he cares that you can't figure out how to beat that boss on that video game/how to do your homework.

He is wisdom.

Ask Him for some!
He delights in you receiving from Him!

Look at this-

Ephesians 4:29-30
"Let no corrupt communication proceed out of your mouth, but only what is good for building others up, that it may minister grace unto the hearers. And do not grieve the Holy Spirit of God, by whom you were sealed for the day of redemption".

Another translation of

Ephesians 4:30
"And do not make God's Holy Spirit sad; for the Spirit is God's mark of ownership on you..."
Do not make the Holy Spirit sad.

What makes the Holy Spirit sad?

Look back at
Ephesians 4:29.
Do not say things that bring people down, but only things that build others up and minister "grace" to the people who hear you speak.

When you say something to someone that is contrary to God's grace, it makes the Holy Spirit sad.

Why is this?

Reflect on everything we have discussed so far.

God wants an intimate relationship with you.

That makes Him happy.

So, wouldn't it only make sense that something that prevents that intimacy would have the opposite effect?

When people come under condemnation, it puts up barriers between themselves and God and prevents that intimacy.
When you tell someone something like; "Yes God loves you but... you should do this, this and this or else he will not listen to your prayers/bless you."

Or "Yes God loves you but... if you continue to do this, He will be angry with you and you should ask Him for Forgiveness before He will continue to bless take part in intimate relationship with you.

" Or even, "God loves you, so you need to change this and do this, or stop doing this, so you can enter into a relationship with Him."

This is contrary to God's grace!

<u>Romans 2:4</u>
says that it is God's goodness that causes people to repent.

It is His blessings, goodness, love and kindness that causes people to repent (the Greek word used for repent in the New Testament is a word that means "to change your mind.") Not judgment.

So, saying that people need to do/change something before God will pour out His blessings on them/have relationship with them, is counterproductive.

His love comes first.

People need to know this so that they can receive it.

No need to pass judgment on people. People know in their heart what is wrong *(Romans 1:18)*.

Instead tell them this; "God loves you, no strings attached.
Even if you never change, you are still His beloved.

He will still have a relationship with you.

He will withhold nothing good from you".
Beloved, you can freely say this because Jesus is the one who earned God's favor for us.

It's not about what people do/don't do.

It's about what Jesus has done.

Titus 3:5
"he saved us, not because of righteous things we had done, but because of his mercy. He saved us through the washing of rebirth

and renewal by the Holy Spirit"

You think your ability to have a relationship with God is because you have this lifestyle, and others, they do not have ability to have relationship with God because they have that lifestyle?

You think this is based on your own good actions?
How dare you try to take credit for what Jesus did?

Is His perfect sacrifice not enough?

Perhaps He only paid for part of it, and you must suffer as well?

No. He took all sin upon Himself.
Jesus said He will NEVER leave you or forsake you!

He means what He says!

Even if you sin or mess something up, He knows that is when you need Him most!

But when you speak things that condemn others, it causes them to feel guilty and they, thinking they are unclean, will back away from Jesus and put up a wall between Jesus and themselves.

It causes them to break that intimacy that Jesus delights in so much!
And what does that do?

It does the opposite of what you were trying to do in the first place.

Because without Jesus, you no longer have the power to

John 8
"go and sin no more".

God's grace is what empowers us not to sin.

Titus 2:12
"What if I'm just not that close to Jesus?'

Maybe you want to sin, but maybe you're just not feeling it, or you don't quite understand totally.

Do not worry about it!!!

He understands. Just focus on His love for you. Your love is a response to His love.

1 John 4:10
"This is love: not that we loved God, but that he loved us..."

His love comes first.

That's the way it works.

Focus on Him loving you.

Meditate on Him loving you at the cross.

Think about the good things He has done for you and begin to praise Him for it.

The more you meditate on His love for you; your love response will come naturally without even trying.

John 8: 9-10
At this, those who heard began to go away one at a time, the older ones first, until only Jesus was left, with the woman still standing there. Then Jesus stood up again and said to the woman, "Where are your accusers?
Didn't even one of them condemn you?
" "No one, sir," she said. "Then neither do I condemn you," Jesus declared.
"Go and sin no more."

"Don't you see how wonderfully kind, tolerant, and patient God is with you?

Does this mean nothing to you?

Can't you see that his kindness that causes you to repent?
<u>Romans 2:4</u>

But now God's way of putting people right with Himself is now revealed.

It has nothing to do with the law, even though the Law of Moses and the prophets gave their witness to it.

God puts people right through their faith in Jesus Christ. God does this to all who believe in Christ, because there is no difference at all: everyone has sinned; we all fall short of God's glorious standard.

But by the gift of God's grace are all put right with Him through Christ Jesus who sets them free.

<u>STEP # 12</u>

Having had a spiritual experience as the result of these steps, I try to carry this message to others and practice these principles in all our affairs.

<u>Galatians 6:1</u>
Brothers, if someone is caught in a sin, you who are spiritual should restore them gently. But watch yourself, or you also may be tempted.

The world is a dark place.
It is filled with sin, pain and despair.
Shadows overwhelm everything.
It seems as if there is no hope.
And despite all this, if you look close enough, you can see a spark of light.
A light that outshines the darkness.

A light that keeps evil at bay.

And before you now it, it grows in strength and evaporates the blackness leaving peace behind.

If there is one thing God wants us to be, it is to be the light in the murky world that surrounds us.

He wants you to shine.

He wants you to overcome fear and sin, to strive and to light the world around you.

You may think you are worthless, without meaning but God loves you enough to put you on this earth with the potential to change it.

Let Gods word be your fuel, let Gods love be your heat, let His wisdom be your air.
With these 3 things you will be a light and you will have purpose.

Darkness may tempt you to burn out, but if God is with you who could stand against you?

With Him at your side no darkness can burn you out!

Without light you will stumble in darkness, but if you walk the path of light no darkness can stop you.

The world is a place of greed and treachery.

Just one light can make a difference.

MY STRUGGLES

Alone and Depressed, once again, all alone, I suppose I must deserve it, I am clingy and annoying, Obnoxious and dense, Rash and silly, Lazy and obsessive, Sometimes I hate myself, I want to draw people in, but only push them away, I cry so much lately, because everything hurts, not meant to be happy, I force my smile, I fake my laugh,

Does anyone notice?

Does anyone care?

It has not "Like Me" to be so,

Depressed? Upset? Angry?

What is 'like me'?

Someone tell me, Because I do not know myself anymore, once again, as before, I am all alone.

ANXIETY, MY NIGHTMARE

Anxiety,
my nightmare It wraps its non-material hands around my neck, clenches just hard enough to disrupt the normal inhale & exhale motion,

but not block it off completely.

It slithers in through my windpipe, and binds me to lay on my kitchen floor in a fetal position.

Other times it pressures me to race into the woods at night time, like there was something terribly frightening to flee from in that very same damned kitchen.
I have no better words to describe it:

it feels like an evil entity strangling me,

only it is not strangling me by the throat,

it is strangling my entire being, my soul.

PTSD LOOKING FOR HOPE

I have Post Traumatic Stress Disorder. I must remember to breathe every time those words come,

I do not want to believe it.

I still cannot believe it.

I remember the first time my

counselor looked at me and told me that my depression and anxiety might be something more.

Great, I thought, what could be worse than this?

Firstly, PTSD is not a disorder that only affects our war heroes, though that is what it is associated with.

My own first thoughts were:

"isn't that a disorder for war veterans or someone who saw war first- hand?

"The truth is there are many causes for Post-Traumatic Stress Disorder,

for example: seeing or experiencing incidents,

such as mugging,

rape,

child abuse,

drug abuse,

illnesses,

car accidents,

plane crashes,

or natural disasters such as hurricanes or earthquakes can all trigger PTSD.

However, not every person who survives a traumatic event develops PTSD, as we all cope differently to terrifying situations.

Sometimes it can take a few months for symptoms to begin to show up or occasionally it can take years before signs of the disorder are clear.

Some people can recover within months, while others experience the symptoms for much longer.

The hardest part for me is accepting the fact that I was traumatized because I had banished any memories to the deepest parts of my mind.

I do not want to remember.

This was my coping mechanism,

I simply pretended it did not exist and that it never happened.

I remember repeatedly telling myself that it was just a nightmare and that I was being silly for thinking it even occurred.

This is not a good coping technique as I spent most of my time obsessing and telling myself that it was all in my head.

That I was just overreacting to those constant nightmares and emotions that swirled around like leftover pudding.

I felt as if I was floating all the time and in fact, I was--I was floating on all the lies I had told myself.

Even this very minute, as I write this, I am pushing back those memories that resurface and stay on the edge of my mind like an oil spill.

I am constantly afraid for my life.

Daytime consists of me never left alone, it does not matter to if someone is a room away, I cannot stand to be alone.

I need to have someone I trust close by and in the same room as me.

Going out into public is one of my biggest fears, it is where I relive what happened the most.

I am afraid of people.

I also have a constant, nagging fear that something terrible will happen and so, I mentally prepare for the worst scenario.

I trust everyone and I trust no one.

At night my symptoms become worse,

I cannot go anywhere without making sure there is light illuminating my path. I need to be able to see everything in front of me,

I wake up groggy and as soon as I flip the light switch I become hyper-vigilante of every noise and movement.

I become jumpy and sprint towards my destination,

always making sure I can reach a weapon if necessary.

There are times when I hear a noise that I become deathly silent,

straining to hear every movement,

and will still be in the same spot for upwards of twenty minutes.

Then I must pick up the nearest object and hold it in a defensive stance,

I will then carefully walk over to the door and open it all the way.

I always look three times to make sure no one is hiding behind the door or around the corner.

I suffer from mild flashbacks and body memories of the events. In other words, I can re-live the moment to the extreme;

I can remember every tiny detail.

I remember how hard my heart would pound, the subtle smells, the noises.

Everything.

Just thinking about it increases my heart rate and I start to shake, it is hard to discuss because it feels like a fresh wound.

High school was the worst for me and I am not talking about the cliques, bullies, and things like that.

Those types of things did not bother me in the least bit, I could take an insult from someone and whisk it away faster than their mouth could move.

On the outside I was strong but on the inside, I was rotting into nothing.

Though, at some point in ninth grade something in me snapped.

I became nervous and anxious all the time;

I could not enjoy anything I used to without racing thoughts of all the horrible things that could happen.

School became a burden because all my thoughts went to everything that could go wrong.

When I say everything, I mean everything.

In school, I used to worry about getting kidnapped as I waited for the bus or that if an intruder came into the school his target would be me because I always felt so helpless.

I lived a nightmare.

I survived it and I am still here but it will not let go.
However, it is easier.

Easier to cope, to tell myself that I am not alone and to make myself believe that someday I will be all right.

Because, one day, it will be all right.

EPILOGUE

Contrary to what some people believe,

Christians can still struggle with things like addiction.

If you are a Christian who struggles with this, keep reading.

Because I believe revelation of Jesus in this area can change your life.

Some things to remember:

You are righteous because of what Jesus did, not because of anything that you did.

Because you are righteous due to Jesus' perfect sacrifice,

and not your own righteousness, you cannot be made unrighteous because of your own unrighteousness.

You did not earn it by your own actions.

You cannot lose it by your own actions.

Titus 3:5

"he saved us, not because of righteous things we had done, but because of his mercy" ...

God is not mad at you.
Addiction is slavery, and Jesus wants you free.

Again,

YOU ARE THE RIGHTEOUSNESS OF GOD IN CHRIST!

Romans 8:1
"There is now no condemnation for those who are in Christ".

This is the Gospel.

It is understanding this that will help you overcome. Through Christ, you are made eternally clean.

You can still sin.

Because your mind and body is not perfect yet.

But you are dead to sin (**Romans 6:11**).

Even when you fall, you fall, in Christ.

You are still in Christ.
And in Christ you are a new creation (**2 Corinthians 5:17**).

And your spirit is completely perfect, sealed and cannot be corrupted. This is how God sees you.

Think of this; Jesus makes you clean, right?

Think of someone who sticks their hand in the mud.

Then its dirty, right? But they can run to a sink and wash it off again.

Then it's clean. You could say that this is like what Christ does for us when we sin right?

When you sin, you are dirty again, but you can run to Jesus to make you clean right?

Not exactly.

Think of the mud and sink scenario again.

You stick your hand in the mud,

then you run to the sink to wash it off
whenever it gets too dirty.

But that is not how it is for those of us
who are in Christ.

For you, it is like this: your hand is
constantly in the sink under the flow of
water.

It cannot get dirty.

Even if you pour mud on it, it is just
automatically washed off from being
under the constant waterfall.

This is your spirit.

You can still sin, because your
mind/body can still run in imperfection,
but your spirit CANNOT
be corrupted.

Christ's blood is continuously forever
making you clean.

You do not need to
run to God and beg for forgiveness
whenever you sin.

When you do this, you are just making
yourself more sin conscious, which
makes you sin more (look at **_Romans
7:7-8_**).

Jesus paid for no condemnation for
you, so you would not have to feel
condemned, in order for you to be free
and ultimately overcome this. Let us
relate this to addiction.

Think of someone who is addicted to
looking at adult websites/films.

You look at the website and then you
know you have messed up.

But you know that God is merciful and
will forgive you, so you can just ask for
forgiveness. But why ask now?
You have already messed up, so you
might as well just finish watching.

If you ask now, you will just continue anyway, then must ask again.

So, you might as well just finish the movie and ask later.

Besides, you will sin more today, so you might as well just wait until the end of the day before you go to bed and then ask for forgiveness for all your sins that day to make sure everything is covered.

You see how messed up that is?

That is why this does not work.

Guilt/shame/condemnation empowers addiction. It does not free you.

You stay stuck in what you are doing.

This is not the kind of freedom Jesus had in mind.

He did not come to earth and die just so,

you could stay doing what you are doing every day, and then at the end of the day ask for forgiveness so you can feel good about yourself!

Jesus wants it gone!

Jesus loves you and wants you to be free! Think of this; you have a friend who is wealthier than you are.

One day this friend buys you a awesome new jacket.

He bought it for you because he loves you. Not because of anything you did.

But it's a gift.

However, it is a lot nicer than what you are used to wearing.

It is something you could never afford on your own.

But then one day, another acquaintance of yours sees you wearing that jacket, and he says "What are you doing wearing that?

That is way too good for you! You do not deserve that!

You cannot afford that!

Take it off, and give it here!
" So then, you timidly lower your head, take off the jacket and hand it over to your accuser saying "Yeah, your right, I cannot afford this.

I am not good enough to wear it.

Here you go." What you did not realize is that your friend, the one who originally bought you this jacket, was standing there and he just saw the whole thing. He runs over to you with hurt in his eyes and says, "What did you do that for?!"

You reply, "I can't afford that Jacket."

Then your friend says, "I know you cannot afford it!

That is why I bought it for you! Do you know what I spent to get that for you?!

It WAS NOT CHEAP! I can't believe you just did that!"

Jesus bought righteousness for you!

Because you could not carry out it on your own apart from Him.

And it WAS NOT CHEAP!

He suffered to a level that you will never understand!

He does not want you to understand it!
Not only the physical suffering of the crucifixion, but the emotional suffering and the spiritual suffering of a God who never knew sin to become sin!

He put His robe of righteousness on you.

This came at a price.
Beloved, you ARE the righteousness of God in Christ!

Through Christ, all your sins are forgiven!

Not just when you ask for forgiveness.

The word "repent" used in the bible in the original Greek is a word that means "to change your mind".

What you need to repent and change your mind about is settling for less than what Jesus bought for you!

Tell Him, "Jesus I am sorry for not putting on your robe of righteousness because I felt that I was not good enough to wear it, as if I could wear it because of something I did/avoided doing.

I realize now that it was because of your perfect obedience at the cross, not my own, that I can say that I am eternally clean.
Thank you for this gift of no condemnation!

I believe I am the righteousness of God through you Christ Jesus because of what you accomplished for me!"

Now back to my example of addiction.

Instead of feeling like you need to run to Jesus to get clean again after you slip up, if you mess up and look at an inappropriate website/film, do not let the accuser accuse you of not being a very good Christian.

Instead, say to yourself "I am the righteousness of God in Christ because Jesus took all of my sin.

Jesus still loves me!

This does not affect God's opinion of me.

Thank you, Jesus, for this grace that I am still your beloved and you will withhold nothing good from me!
" Say and rehearse these things out loud whenever you are watching, smoking, or whatever it is that you do. Say these things no matter how many times you do it.

No condemnation is the key for being able to "go and sin no more".

Look at ***John 8***.

When the prostitute was brought before Jesus, the last thing He said to her was "I don't condemn you.

Go and sin no more." He said this because He knew He was going to pay the price for her sin on the cross.

Beloved, it is easy to sin against hard cold stone tablets that say THOU SHALL NOT DO THIS!

But it is difficult to sin against a beautiful savior who loves you.
"For God has revealed his grace for the salvation of all people.

That grace instructs us to give up ungodly living and worldly lusts and to live self-controlled, upright, and godly lives in this world," (***Titus 2:11-12***).

God's grace gives you the power to not sin.

But if you are still condemning yourself/accepting condemnation from others, and not believing in God's grace that you are clean, then you are not using that power, even though it is available.
One more thing.
Pray in the Holy Spirit.

As His precious beloved child, God wants you to have the supernatural power you need to overcome anything, including addiction. Remember, you are a child of God, not of the world.

You are in the world, not of it.

You don't have to operate in the way that the people of the world do.

Why pray in the Holy Spirit?

When you pray in the Holy Spirit, it is your spirit, not your mind that prays (***1 Corinthians 14:14***).

It is the Holy Spirit who gives you the words. If you've never used this gift before, ask God to fill you with this power right now.

This is a gift, just like salvation. All you must do is ask for it, and you don't have to do anything to earn it.

If you've asked, and believed that you have received, then you've got it.

When you pray in the spirit, you are praying the perfect will of God.
You are speaking supernatural power and "edifying" yourself or "building

yourself up" (***1 Corinthians 14:4***).

If there is anything that addiction has done to damage your mind/body, the Holy Spirit knows what to do to fix it.

He knows exactly what you need.

When you feel like you want to look at an adult website/other addiction, start praying in the supernatural prayer language that the Lord gives you.

When your body is telling you that you need to do something that is harmful, the Holy Spirit knows what needs to be done to correct this.

He is your personal Helper.

Give your cares to Him and let Him take care of you.

Made in the USA
Coppell, TX
07 June 2021

56999504R00056